Anonymous

Before the throne

Daily devotions for a child

Anonymous

Before the throne
Daily devotions for a child

ISBN/EAN: 9783337257897

Printed in Europe, USA, Canada, Australia, Japan

Cover: Foto ©Andreas Hilbeck / pixelio.de

More available books at **www.hansebooks.com**

BEFORE

The Throne;

OR,

DAILY DEVOTIONS

FOR A CHILD.

Hearken unto the voice of my cry, my King, and my God: for unto thee will I pray.—*Psalm* v. 2.

New York:

M. W. DODD, No. 506 BROADWAY.

1869.

Edward O. Jenkins,

PRINTER AND STEREOTYPER,

No. 20 North William St.

PREFACE.

SOME months since when visiting a dear friend, her little girl begged the privilege of sharing Auntie's room, on the first night, with the added request that I would undress her and put her to bed. When ready for bed, the child simply knelt at my side, and folding her hands in my lap, waited for prompting in her evening prayer. Quite ignorant of her usual form, I involuntarily began, "Our Father which art in heaven." Slowly and reverently the childish voice followed mine through that sweet prayer, softly adding the familiar "Now I lay me," etc. Tired from my journey, I did not return to the circle below stairs, but after a little quiet reading and my own devotions, I softly sought the pillow, where I supposed my pet was fast asleep. But no. She at once said, "Hug me up tight,

Auntie ;" and, then, coaxingly patting my cheek, asked, " What do *you* pray for, Auntie ? Tell me, what do you pray for ?" Here was a little child not far past her fourth birthday, who already felt that prayer was something more than a form of words, and that different people must have different wants to bring before the Throne.

A desire to help such little ones to a knowledge of the still waters and green pastures of communion with our Father in heaven, has been a principal motive in the preparation of this little work.

BROOKLYN, 1868.

Our Father, who art in heaven, Hallowed be thy Name. Thy kingdom come. Thy will be done on earth, As it is in heaven. Give us this day our daily bread. And forgive us our trespasses, As we forgive those who trespass against us. And lead us not into temptation; But deliver us from evil; For thine is the kingdom, and the power, and the glory, for ever and ever. Amen.

First Sunday.

REMEMBER the Sabbath-day, to keep it holy.

Six days shalt thou labour, and do all thy work :

But the seventh day is the Sabbath of the Lord thy God : in it thou shall not do any work, thou, nor thy son, nor thy daughter, thy man-servant, nor thy maid-servant, nor thy cattle, nor thy stranger that is within thy gates :

For in six days the Lord made heaven and earth, the sea, and all that in them is, and rested the seventh day : wherefore, the Lord blessed the Sabbath-day, and hallowed it —Exodus xx. 8–11.

Morning Prayer.

HOLY Lord God who made heaven and earth, Thou hast kept me in safety, and brought me to see the light of another Sabbath day ; help me to remember that it is Thy day, and to keep it holy to Thee. Put far away from me sinful thoughts and wishes, that so I may not do unholy deeds. If I go to Thy house, or to Sunday-school, do Thou, O God! go with me to keep me in Thy fear. Teach me how to worship Thee in spirit and in truth. Make me quiet and attentive, watching for some words for me, though I am but a little child among Thy worshipers. Fill my heart to-day with such love as Jesus had when He was on earth. Take my first best love to Thyself, and then make me loving to all Thy creatures. Especially, put love in my heart to-day towards all little children who are not taught to know and love Jesus. Have pity upon such; send them teachers, and give them Thy Holy Spirit to convert them unto Thee. Bless all ministers and teachers who shall speak for Thee to-day. May Thy kingdom come, and the whole world be made to love and serve Thee, the ever-blessed Father, Son and Holy Spirit! Amen.

Evening Prayer.

HIS has been Thy day O God! and now at its close, before I lie down to sleep, I would stop and think how I have kept it. Not without sin, for even my thoughts are sinful; my lips are always ready to speak light words, and my hands and feet ready to do unholy acts. Forgive me that I have loved these, my sins, better than I have loved Thee. Teach me the great wickedness of sin, even of what I call little sins. Make me to know that of myself, and in my own strength, I can neither stop sinning, nor take away its stain and guilt from my soul. Then grant me Thy grace and help, that I may fight against evil and grow every day more like a Christian child. Although I have not remembered to keep this day all holy to Thee, I pray Thee yet to let some sweet influences go with me through this week, making me better than if I had not had it. Keep me in peace and safety to-night.

Watch over me during its hours. Refresh me by my sleep, and when I wake, fill my heart with love to Thee. For Jesus' sake I ask it. Amen.

Hymn.

HOW sweet is the Sabbath, the morning of
   rest,
 The day of the week which I ought to
   love best;
The morning my Saviour arose from the tomb,
And took from the grave all its terror and gloom.

Then let me be thoughtful and prayerful to-day,
And not spend a moment in trifling or play;
Remembering these seasons were graciously given
To teach me to seek, and prepare me for heaven.

Instruct me, my Saviour! a child though I be,
I am not too young to be noticed by Thee;
Renew all my heart, keep me firm in Thy ways,
I would love Thee, and serve Thee, and give Thee
   the praise.

Monday.

HE Lord is thy keeper : the Lord is thy shade upon thy right hand.

The sun shall not smite thee by day, nor the moon by night.

The Lord shall preserve thee from all evil : He shall preserve thy soul.

The Lord shall preserve thy going out and thy coming in from this time forth, and even for ever more.—PSALM cxxi. 5–8.

Morning Prayer.

LAID me down in peace and slept, I awaked because Thou O Lord ! didst watch over and care for me. Fill my heart with thankful love for all Thy mercies. Every day of my life is full of Thy kindness and love. I thank Thee for all ; for life and home, for friends and playmates, for food and clothing. And, above all, I thank Thee for sending Thine only Son to die to save sinners, of whom I am one. Lord God! show me how great is Thy gift to me, and help me to make the only return I can, and give Thee myself. Keep me to-day in all my ways. Save me from pain and harm if it please Thee. Help me to remember Thee. Give me Thy grace in my heart. Help me in all my duties, making me true and faithful in doing them. Bless me in my plays. Make me kind and gentle with my playmates. Bless them with me. Bless too my parents, brothers and sisters, and all my friends. Bless the whole world with Thy salvation, and Thine shall be the praise and the glory for ever! Amen.

Evening Prayer.

THOU great and glorious God! who dost never sleep, because Thou art never tired, keep a watch over me, I pray Thee, while I rest in sleep. I will

put my trust in Thee, and not be afraid,
for no harm can come nigh me when Thou
art my keeper. Send down Thy peace and
love into my heart, and fill my mind with
pleasant, holy thoughts. Put away all angry, fretful, wicked feelings from my heart,
and give me kind and gentle love toward
every one. More than all give me much
love and thankfulness to Thee, who art
blessing me so richly and loving me so
graciously. Forgive all in me that Thou
canst not love, and take away from me all
love for sin that is displeasing to Thee.
Make me like Jesus, for Jesus' sake!
Amen.

Hymn.

JESUS, Lord, to Thee I pray,
  Guide and guard me through this day.

As the shepherd tends the sheep,
Lord, me safe from evil keep.

Keep my feet from every snare,
Keep me with Thy watchful care:

All my little wants supply,
If I live or if I die.

And when life, O Lord! is past,
Take me to Thyself at last!

Tuesday.

I LOVE them that love me : and those that seek me early shall find me.—Prov. viii. 17.

And ye shall seek me, and find me, when ye shall search for me with all your heart.—Jer. xxix. 13.

A new heart also will I give you, and a new spirit will I put within you : and I will take away the stony heart out of your flesh, and I will give you an heart of flesh. Ezek. xxxvi. 26.

Morning Prayer.

GREAT and holy God, who hast said, I love them that love me, and those that seek me early shall find me, teach me to love Thee, that so Thou mayest love me. Give me, I pray Thee an earnest wish to seek Thee, that so

I may find Thee. Grant me Thy Holy Spirit and make this the true prayer of my heart, as well as words upon my lips.

I thank Thee O Lord for thy many blessings to me. May Thy loving-kindness ever be about me. Keep a kind watch over me this day, and keep me not only from danger and hurt, but from temptation and wrong doing. Make me obedient, truthful and kind. Give the same blessings I ask for myself to my friends. Make us all Thy friends. Do for us more and better than I can ask or think. Hear my prayer, O God, forgive all my sins, and accept of me for the dear Saviour's sake. Amen.

Evening Prayer.

DEAR Jesus, who dost never send away any who come to Thee, I, a little one, would try to come to Thee to-night. Thou lovest little ones, love me. Thou carest for little ones, care for me. Thou blessest little ones, bless me.

Thou forgivest little ones, forgive me. Thou savest little ones, save me. I am small, and weak, and ignorant, and sinful. Thou art great, and strong, and wise, and holy. Thou art love, too, all love. Thou hast room in Thy great, strong, wise heart for foolish, sinful little ones. Let me creep in, and hide in Thy love, and in the shadow of Thy cross. Because Thou hast died for sinners, and didst so prove Thy love to them, when they did not love Thee, I am not afraid to come and ask Thee to love and pardon me. Wash me in Thy blood, clean and pure from all sin. Clothe me with Thy righteousness. Forgive all my sins. Bless me while I live. Help me to live in Thy fear and to Thy glory. Accept and save me at last, to praise Thee in heaven forever. Amen.

Hymn.

LAY my sins on Jesus,
  The spotless Lamb of God;
He bears them all, and frees us
  From the accursed load.

I bring my guilt to Jesus,
  To wash my crimson stains,
White in his blood most precious,
  'Till not a spot remains.

I lay my wants on Jesus,
  All fulness dwells in him,
He healeth my diseases,
  He doth my soul redeem.

Wednesday.

BUT thou, when thou prayest, enter into thy closet, and when thou hast shut thy door, pray to thy Father which is in secret; and thy Father, which seeth in secret, shall reward thee openly.—MATT. vi. 6.

Watch and pray that ye enter not into temptation.—MATT. xxvi. 41.

In everything by prayer and supplication with thanksgiving let your requests be made known unto God.—PHIL. iv. 6.

Pray without ceasing.—I THESS. v. 17.

Morning Prayer.

O GOD! help me to come before Thee now in prayer humbly and reverently, as I ought to come to worship the great God, who is King over all worlds. Yet make me loving and free in asking of Thee, my Heavenly Father, such things as a child may ask of a kind parent. May I pray unto Thee from my heart, really wanting what I ask, lest I should mock Thee with unmeaning words. Forgive, I pray Thee, my sins against Thy love. Wash them all away with the blood of Thy dear Son, whom Thou gavest to die for sinners. O Lord! how constantly I sin and do that which I know is wrong and displeasing to Thee. What can I do to become pure and holy? It is of no use for me to try to make myself good. Do Thou, O Lord! do it for me. Give me a new heart. Keep me in mind of Thee, Thy love and Thy commandments. Lord, save me, or I perish. For Thy great love's sake I ask it. Bless all for whom I should pray; the poor, the sick, sinners, all my friends. Do for them all more and better than I can ask Thee, and Thine shall be all the praise and the glory for ever! Amen.

Evening Prayer.

LMIGHTY God! Thou hast kept me through yet another day. I am alive because Thou hast not once forgotten me. Forgive me that I have so often forgotten Thee. Forgive and bless me for Jesus' sake. Kind and loving Jesus pity me in my weakness and sin. Make me careful to please Thee. Draw me to Thee by Thy love. Make me like unto Thee, because I love Thee. Lord, show me Thyself. Teach me to know Thee, and then I cannot help loving Thee. Make me true and sincere in asking this of Thee, and answer my prayer in love. Take me in Thy care this night. Let Thy peace be with me and Thy watchful eye over me while I sleep, and when I awake may I be still praising Thee. Hear my prayer, not because I am good or worthy, but because Thou art love! Amen.

Hymn.

DEAR Jesus, let Thy pitying eye
Look kindly down on me;
A sinful, weak and helpless child,
I come Thy child to be.

O blessed Saviour, take my heart,
This sinful heart of mine,
And wash it clean in every part;
Make me a child of Thine!

For Thou hast said, " Forbid them not,
Let children come to me."
I hear Thy voice, and now, dear Lord,
I come Thy child to be.

Thursday.

IN this was manifested the Love of God toward us, because that God sent his only begotten Son into the world, that we might live through Him. Herein is love, not that we loved God, but that he loved us, and sent His Son to be the propitiation for our sins.

We love him, because he first loved us.—1 JOHN iv. 9, 10, 19.

But God commendeth his love toward us, in that while we were yet sinners, Christ died for us.—ROMANS v. 8.

Morning Prayer.

GREAT and holy Lord, who art a King in heaven, how can I a little, sinful child dare to come before Thee? Let me hide myself in the love of Thy dear Son, and beg that for

Jesus' sake, Thou wilt hear my prayer. O Lord, Thou art very pure and righteous and canst not love anything that is unholy, but art angry with the wicked every day. Be pleased to wash me in Christ's blood which cleanseth from all sin, and fill my heart with right and holy thoughts, that so Thou mayest love me, and dwell in my heart. Do Thou be my guide and my strength. Show me what is right, and help me to choose it. Help me to keep a watch upon my lips, that they speak no angry or disobedient words. Keep my hands and feet from deeds and paths that displease Thee. Teach me to be gentle, loving, truthful and obedient. Fill my heart with love to Thee, and to all around me. Keep me from all evil and danger. Bless with me all my friends, and all for whom I should pray, and bring us to praise Thee at last in heaven for Jesus' sake. Amen.

Evening Prayer.

TENDER Saviour who didst take little children in Thy arms to bless them, when Thou wast on earth, bless me, a little child, who seeks Thy loving care through the dark hours of the night. I thank Thee for the day now gone. Help me to keep some good from its lessons. Forgive every sin that I have done, and while I come to Thee every day asking Thee to forgive, let me not be satisfied with that, but give me grace every day to try and get the victory over my sinful habits. Give me an earnest wish in my heart to be holy, true, gentle and good. May I wish it so much, that I shall strive with all my might to obtain it; and not with my might only, but with the strength Thou wilt give to all who ask Thee. I give myself and all whom I love into Thy care to-night. Do for us all as seemeth good in Thy sight. Accept us and save us for Thy name's sake. Amen.

Hymn.

JESUS, tender Shepherd, hear me;
  Bless Thy little Lamb to-night:
Through the darkness be Thou near me,
  Watch my sleep till morning light.

All this day Thy hand has led me,
  And I thank Thee for Thy care;
Thou hast clothed me, warmed me, fed me,
  Listen to my evening prayer.

Let my sins be all forgiven;
  Bless the friends I love so well:
Take me, when I die, to heaven
  Happy there with Thee to dwell.

Friday.

THE Lord is my shepherd; I shall not want.

He maketh me to lie down in green pastures: He leadeth me beside the still waters.

He restoreth my soul: He leadeth me in the paths of righteousness for His name's sake.

Yea, though I walk through the valley of the shadow of death, I will fear no evil: for Thou art with me; Thy rod and Thy staff they comfort me.—PSALM xxiii. 1–4.

Morning Prayer.

ALMIGHTY God! infinite in power and holiness, but just as infinite in goodness and love, I would seek Thy grace and favor, trusting in Thy promise, that they who seek shall find. Attend unto my prayer; hear and answer me in love. Take me into Thy kind, wise care

and keeping this day.   Go with me where
I go, stay with me where I stay.   Save me
from danger ; supply all my wants ; deliver me from temptation and sin ; keep
me from all evil.   I am only a little child,
make me one of the lambs of Thy fold.   I
am weak, do Thou be my strength.   I am
ignorant, do Thou teach me true wisdom.
I am a sinner, wash me in Christ's blood,
and forgive and love me for His sake.
Bless all my friends this day.   Thou dost
see and know them all.   Love them all,
too, and make them sharers with me in
Thy redeeming and forgiving love.   And
we will give all the praise and glory of our
salvation to the only wise and true God,
Father, Son and Holy Ghost, for ever.
Amen.

Evening Prayer.

DEAR Saviour ! grant me, I pray
Thee, Thy blessing as I go to my
rest this night.   Then I will lay
me down in peace and sleep, for Thou,

Lord, makest me to dwell in safety. How great is this Thy love to me, that Thou dost permit a sinful little child to seek Thy favor, trust in Thy grace, and hide in Thy love. Make me to know more perfectly the greatness of Thy love, and teach me to love Thee with all my heart in return for Thy goodness to me. Forgive in mercy the ill that I have done this day. Take away all sin from my heart, that I may go to sleep at peace with myself, the world, and Thee. Take care of me through the dark night, and not of me only, but of all my friends, and of all for whom Thou wouldst have me pray. Bless, love, and keep us all in Thine own tender care, and Thine shall be all honor, praise and glory for ever. Amen.

Hymn.

NOTHING either great or small,
Remains for me to do;
Jesus died and paid it all—
Yes, all the debt I owe.

When He from His lofty throne,
  Stooped down to do and die ;
Everything was fully done ;
  "'Tis finished !" was His cry.

Till to Jesus' work you cling,
  Alone by simple faith,
" Doing " is a deadly thing,
  Your " doing " ends in death.

Saturday.

REMEMBER now thy Creator in the days of thy youth, while the evil days come not, nor the years draw nigh, when thou shalt say, I have no pleasure in them ;

While the sun, or the light, or the moon, or the stars, be not darkened, nor the clouds return after the rain :

Or ever the silver cord be loosed, or the golden bowl be broken, or the pitcher be broken at the fountain, or the wheel broken at the cistern.

Then shall the dust return to the earth as it was : and the spirit shall return unto God who gave it.—ECCL. xii. 1, 2, 6, 7.

Morning Prayer.

O GOD ! early this morning help me to worship Thee with a true heart, and ask Thee to take care of me and guide me through another day. Thou art angry with the wicked every day, and I am a weak and sinful little child. Even when I think I am very good, Thou art so pure and holy that my sins are very hateful in Thy sight. I am not able of myself to do any good thing, but I come to Thee for help. Grant me, I pray Thee, Thy Holy Spirit to keep me from sinning. Thou who didst say, Suffer little children to come unto me, turn me not away because I am sinful, but in Thy great love forgive my wickedness, and give me a new heart that shall love and serve Thee. Grant me all the blessings and happiness Thou seest best for me this day; and not to me only, but to all whom I love, and all for whom I should pray. For Jesus' sake I ask it. Amen.

Evening Prayer.

O LORD! Thou hast kept me safely through another week, and now at its close I come to thank Thee for Thy loving care. Sleeping or waking Thou hast never forgotten me, but hast kept me from dangers seen and unseen. Yet, O Lord! how often have I forgotten Thee, and done that which I knew was displeasing to Thee. Wilt Thou forgive this my sin, and teach me to remember Thee in my youth. Dear Saviour! make me so to know and feel Thy great love to sinners, that I cannot help keeping Thee in mind because I love Thee. Help me to pray with all my heart for Thy love and pardon. Prepare me now for Thy holy Sabbath. Help me to put away all thoughts of my play, and every day duties and pleasures, and to keep the day holy to Thee. Now I lay me down to sleep, I pray the Lord my soul to keep. If I should die before I wake, I pray the Lord my soul to take, for Jesus' sake. Amen.

Hymn.

FEEBLE, helpless, how shall I
  Learn to live and learn to die?
    Who, O God! my guide shall be?
Who shall lead Thy child to Thee?

Blessed Father! gracious One!
Thou hast sent Thy holy Son;
He will give the light I need,
He my trembling steps will lead.

Thus in deed, and thought, and word,
Led by Jesus Christ the Lord,
In my weakness thus shall I
Learn to live, and learn to die.

Second Sunday.

LESS the Lord, O my soul : and all that is within me, bless His holy name.

Bless the Lord, O my soul, and forget not all His benefits :

Who forgiveth all thine iniquities ; who healeth all thy diseases ;

Who redeemeth thy life from destruction ; who crowneth thee with loving kindness and tender mercies ;

Who satisfieth thy mouth with goods things ; so that thy youth is renewed like the eagle's.— Psalm ciii. 1—5.

Morning Prayer.

"BLESS the Lord, O my soul, and all that is within me, bless His holy name." Make this, Heavenly Father, the true feeling of my heart on this Thy holy day. Thy loving kindness to me is very great. All that I have comes from Thee, not because I deserve anything, but because Thou dost so love me. I thank Thee for this Thy great love. That Thou dost supply all my wants and keep me alive and in safety. But, dear Saviour! more than all else I thank Thee for Thy best gift, even Thine own self to die for sin. Make me to know the value of this great thing that Thou hast done for sinners. Give me grace to accept Thy love and sacrifice; to believe on Thee; to serve Thee in all my ways, and to look to Thee for pardon, peace and eternal safety. Keep me in Thy fear and love to-day, not thinking my own thoughts, or doing my own pleasure, but lovingly, meekly and humbly doing Thy will and keeping this day holy to the Lord. Give to the whole world the blessings I enjoy. Save sinners and bring them to love Thee in return for Thy great love to them. I ask and offer all in the name and for the sake of Jesus Christ. Amen.

Evening Prayer.

EAVENLY Father! make me quiet and serious as I come to Thee for Thy blessing at the close of this Sabbath-day. Make me feel that Thou art really here with me, seeing me, though I cannot see Thee, hearing me, though I cannot hear Thee, knowing all my thoughts before I speak them, or even know them myself. And may this knowledge of Thy presence and power be a pleasant thing to me; not because I am holy and fit to appear before Thee, or am worthy of Thy notice, but because, for Thy Son's sake, Thou art willing to be my Friend and Father. Forgive, I pray Thee, all that Thou hast seen wrong in me this day. Make me sorry for my sins, and truly in earnest in seeking to be free from them. I give myself into Thy holy keeping. Be pleased to watch over me, to take care of me, to bless me, to forgive and love me. And when my life on earth shall end, take me to Thyself in the happy land, for Jesus' sake I ask it. Amen.

Hymn.

LORD of the Sabbath, I rejoice
　　Thine holy day to see;
　　May I, assisted by Thy grace,
Begin this week with Thee.

I go this day to hear Thy Word,
　　To sing, to pray, and praise;
To learn of Thee, my gracious Lord,
　　Religion's pleasant ways.

Oh, may the Holy Spirit bless
　　These sacred means of grace,
That I may learn Thy righteousness
　　And seek in youth Thy face!

Monday.

IF we confess our sins, He is faithful and just to forgive us our sins, and to cleanse us from all unrighteousness.—1 JOHN i. 9.

And if any man sin, we have an advocate with the Father, Jesus Christ the righteous.—1 JOHN ii. 1.

Wherefore He is able also to save them to the uttermost that come unto God by Him, seeing He ever liveth to make intercession for them.— HEB. vii. 25.

Morning Prayer.

IT seems a strange thing to me, O God! that when I kneel down to pray to Thee, Thou art very near me, yet I cannot see Thee, or touch Thee. That though I cannot hear Thee, Thou dost hear every word I say, and not only so, but dost know my thoughts, and wheth-

er I mean what I say. I do not understand
it at all. Will Thou please to teach me all
I need to know, and give me a heart ready
to believe if I cannot understand. This
one thing I can understand: Thou dost
love sinners very much. Help me, a sinner, to love Thee since Thou hast first
loved me; to love Thee better than all the
world beside; to try to please Thee; to
give Thee my heart; to win others to love
Thee too. Show me to-day how I may
prove my love to Thee. Show me what
to do for Jesus, and make me willing to
do anything I can for Thee. In all my
life here, do Thou, I pray Thee, fit me for
a life in heaven where I shall serve, praise
and love Thee for ever. Amen.

Evening Prayer.

BE pleased, O God! to bless a little
child who seeks to worship Thee
this night. Take away all sinful
thoughts from my mind, that I may go to

sleep in peace. I thank Thee for having kept me safe through another day, and pray Thee to forgive all my evil ways. Show me how great is my wickedness before Thee, and help me to try to please Thee in everything, even in my little duties and plays. Forgive me if I have been unkind or selfish to-day with my playmates. Give me true love in my heart toward all I meet. Forgive all disobedience, anger and ugliness. Make me meek, gentle and holy, the dear Saviour's little child. Give me an earnest wish in my heart to be like Jesus. I commit myself to Thee, dear Saviour! While I sleep, Thou wilt wake. Please to watch over me and my friends, and keep us from danger. Love us always, and teach us to love and serve Thee. And Thine shall be all praise for ever. Amen.

Hymn.

I THINK, when I read that sweet story of old,
  When Jesus was here among men,
    How He called little children as lambs to
    His fold,
  I should like to have been with them then.

I wish that His hands had been placed on my
    head,
  That His arm had been thrown around me,
And that I might have seen His kind look, when
    He said,
  "Let the little ones come unto me."

Yet still to His footstool in prayer I may go,
  And ask for a share in His love;
And if I thus earnestly seek Him below,
  I shall see Him and hear Him above.

Tuesday.

AND they brought young children to Him, that He should touch them; and His disciples rebuked those that brought them.

But when Jesus saw it, He was much displeased, and said unto them, Suffer the little children to come unto me, and forbid them not: for of such is the kingdom of God.

Verily, I say unto you, Whosoever shall not receive the kingdom of God as a little child, he shall not enter therein.

And He took them up in His arms, put His hands upon them, and blessed them.—MARK x. 13–16.

Morning Prayer.

LORD God! who dwellest in heaven, but dost love and care for the people of this earth, hear me, I pray Thee, as I offer Thee a child's prayer. Loving Saviour! Thou didst receive and bless little children during Thy life on earth, and didst never turn them away from Thee. Receive and bless me now, and help me to come to Thee aright. I ask Thee for a new heart, that shall love Thee more than anything else. Lord, I cannot love and serve Thee aright of myself. I come to Thee for help. Do not turn me away, but give me what Thou seest I need. For Thy name's sake, forgive my sins and keep me from sinning. Make me gentle, obedient, truthful and kind. Fill my heart with thankful love to Thee for all Thy goodness to me, and give me love toward all my companions, not only toward those who love me, but to all. Hear my prayer, O God! Forgive all I have asked wrong, or in a wrong spirit. In mercy give me all I need that I have not asked, and so keep me till death for Christ's sake! Amen.

Evening Prayer.

NTO Thee, O Lord! do I lift up my prayer. Come very near unto me, that I may feel Thee here, and worship truly and with my heart in Thy sight. I praise Thee, dear Saviour! for Thy love to me, as shown in every day of my life. That Thou dost not leave me to myself, but dost watch over and keep me all the day long, and through all the dark, still night. When I cannot take care of myself, Thou dost not forget me. When I sleep, Thou art awake and still guarding me. Fill my heart with love and thankfulness to Thee for all Thy mercies. Loving Thee may I love Thy ways. Forgive all my sins, and take away the love of sinning. Make me Thy child, meek, obedient, loving and happy. I give myself into Thy keeping this night. May I rest sweetly in Thy care. Love, I pray Thee, all whom I love. Grant to them the same blessings

I ask for myself. Make them all happy in Thy love. Save us all from sin and danger. Bring us to see the light of another day, if it be Thy will. And when we die, may we live in heaven to sing Thy praises with the holy angels. Amen.

Hymn.

MY Father! when I come to Thee,
I would not only bend the knee,
But with my spirit seek Thy face—
With my whole heart desire Thy grace.

I plead the name of Thy dear Son,
All He has said, all He has done;
Oh, may I feel His love for me,
Who died, from sin to set me free!

To guide me, Lord, be ever nigh;
My sins forgive, my wants supply;
With favor crown my youthful days,
And my whole life shall speak Thy praise.

Wednesday.

O LORD! Thou hast searched me and known me.

Thou knowest my down-sitting and mine up-rising, Thou understandest my thought afar off.

Thou compassest my path and my lying down, and art acquainted with all my ways.

For there is not a word in my tongue, but, lo! O Lord! Thou knowest it altogether.

Search me, O God! and know my heart: try me and know my thoughts.

And see if there be any wicked way in me, and lead me in the way everlasting.—PSALM cxxxix. 1-4, 23, 24.

Morning Prayer.

I THANK Thee, O Lord! my Heavenly Father, that Thou hast kept me in safety through the night and brought me to the light of another day.

And now, early this morning before I go to my work or my play, I come to Thee and ask Thee to watch over me this day. To keep me from all harm and danger, and more than all to keep me from sin. Fill my heart with holy fear and love for Thee, so shall I do Thy will and add to Thy glory in all my ways. Heavenly Father pity me in my weakness, and love me in my sinfulness. Teach me Thy way, and do Thou be the guide of my youth. Bless me to-day in all I do. If it please Thee, make it a happy day to me. Forgive all my sins, only for the sake of Thy dear Son who died to save sinners. Bless and take care of all whom I love, and save us all in glory to praise the Father, Son, and Holy Ghost for ever. Amen.

Evening Prayer.

KIND and tender Jesus who dost love little children, even when they do not love Thee, and who didst die for them as well as for grown people, I am sure that Thou lovest me; help me to love Thee. Help me to give myself to Thee. Make me Thy little child growing every day more like Thee. I beg Thee to-night for pardon for all my sins. Dear Jesus! I am so ready to sin, so easily tempted, I am discouraged with ever trying to be good. I ask Thee to-night not to let me give up trying, but to show me how to try aright. Help me to put my trust in Thee, and look to Thee for strength. Take away my sins. Wash me white and clean in Thy blood. For Thy dear name's sake have mercy on me. Bless me to-night. Watch over me while I sleep; refresh and strengthen me if it be Thy will. Wake me, well and happy in a new day, and keep me always in Thy love and fear, and I will praise Thee for ever. Amen.

Hymn.

JESUS, Saviour, pity me,
Hear me when I cry to Thee;
I've a very naughty heart,
Full of sin in every part;
I can never make it good,
Wilt Thou wash me in Thy blood?

When I try to do Thy will,
Sin is in my bosom still;
And I soon do something bad
That makes me sorrowful and sad;
Who could help or comfort give
If Thou didst not bid me live?

Though I cannot cease from guilt,
Thou canst help me, and Thou wilt;
Since Thy blood for me was shed,
Crowned with thorns Thy blessed head;
Thou, who loved and suffered so,
Ne'er wilt bid me from Thee go.

Thursday.

FOR God so loved the world, that He gave His only begotten Son, that whosoever believeth in Him should not perish, but have everlasting life.

For God sent not His Son into the world to condemn the world; but that the world through Him might be saved.

He that believeth on Him is not condemned: but he that believeth not is condemned already, because he hath not believed in the name of the only begotten Son of God.—JOHN iii. 16–18.

Morning Prayer.

O GOD! Thou art the only wise and true God, how can I dare speak to Thee! Only because Thou didst so love the world as to give Thine only Son to die for sinners. Make me very much in earnest when I pray to Thee. I come this morning to ask for Thy blessing to go with me through this day, not only for the blessing that should keep me in safety and supply my daily wants, but for the blessing that shall keep me from sin and help me to do right. As my need may be this day, I pray Thee give me strength. Strength to be faithful and true, strength to take up any cross Thou givest me to bear, strength to love and serve Thee. Let me never be ashamed to be known as a Christian child, but give me grace meekly to bear Thy name and live to Thy glory. If it please Thee, Father in Heaven, make this a very happy day to me. May I do my duties well and cheerfully, and may my playtime be glad and joyful. Bless with me all for whom I should pray, my parents, brothers and sisters, my play-mates and everybody. Bless the whole world and fill it with Thy love, for Christ's sake. Amen.

Evening Prayer.

DEAR God! I thank Thee for letting me live through another day. I thank Thee for all its pleasures and blessings. If it please Thee I want Thy blessing now the last thing this day. Forgive every sinful thought, word and act, everything I have said or done that I ought not, everything I have left undone that I ought to have done. Make me more careful another day to do right. Take care of me while I sleep. Keep me free from sickness and harm. When I awake watch over and keep me still from danger and hurt, and from the evil that is in the world. Grant the same blessings to all who are near and dear to me. Be a friend to all my friends. Love all whom I love. Bless all for whom I should pray. And to Thee, Father, Son, and Holy Spirit, one great God, shall be all praise for ever. Amen.

Hymn.

JESUS, let a little child
　　Humbly at Thy footstool pray;
　Thou who art so meek and mild,
Stoop and teach me what to say.

Show me what I ought to be,
　Make me every evil shun;
Ever may I look to Thee,
　Ever in Thy footsteps run.

Jesus, all my sins forgive,
　Make me lowly, pure in heart;
For Thy glory may I live,
　And at death go where Thou art.

Friday.

B E kindly affectioned one to another with brotherly love ; in honor preferring one another.—ROM. xii. 10.

And be ye kind one to another, tender hearted, forgiving one another, even as God for Christ's sake hath forgiven you.—EPH. iv. 32.

Forbearing one another, and forgiving one another, if any man hath a quarrel against any : even as Christ forgave you, so also do ye.—COL. iii. 13.

A soft answer turneth away wrath : but grievous words stir up anger.—PROV. xv. 1.

Morning Prayer.

O THOU great and holy Lord God! whom I cannot know or understand; whose life has had no beginning, and will have no end ; whom no eye hath seen or can see, but who Thyself seest all creatures and know est all things. I thank Thee that in Thy greatness Thou hast with love remembered sinful man, and taught us to call Thee our Father. I come to Thee this morning to beg that Thy blessing may make this day a good and happy one to me. Gentle and loving Holy Spirit come into my heart, I pray Thee, and so fill it with Thy sweet influences that there may be no room in it for unholy desires and wrong motives. Teach me the ways of the Lord, so shall my life show forth Thy praise. I pray Thee especially for grace to-day to do my duty to those around me. Make me an obedient child, a faithful scholar, a helpful friend, a cheerful playmate. Keep me from idleness, quarrels, disobedience and all naughtiness. Help me to remember that this morning I have called Thee, not my Father, but our Father, and that all whom I meet are objects of Thy love and care, even as I am, and may this thought make me gentle, loving and peaceful. Forgive all my sins, and deliver me from all evil. In Jesus' name, and for His sake only, I offer this my prayer. Amen.

Evening Prayer.

BLESS me, Heavenly Father! yet once more I pray Thee, and give me Thy sweet peace in my heart as I lie down to sleep. I will not be afraid of any evil thing, for Thou, O Lord! dost keep me. Thou dost never sleep, nor forget, nor grow weary. In the darkness Thou dost watch over and guard me, and when I awake I am still with Thee. Make me very glad that Thou art always so near, so strong, so loving, so careful for me. Keep me mindful that Thou, God! seest me, then shall I be careful not to displease Thee. Make me thus careful, not because I am afraid of Thee, but because I love Thee too well to wish to grieve Thee with naughty ways. Forgive me all my sins of the day that is now gone. Hide Thy

face from them, and for Jesus' sake blot
them out of Thy book. Bless me and
keep me all my life long. Make it a happy
and useful life, spent in Thy fear and love
and to Thy glory. In the dear Saviour's
name I ask all. Amen.

Hymn.

FATHER! when, with childlike feeling,
   I would come to Thee in prayer,
   Simple words my thoughts revealing,
Wilt Thou lend a listening ear?
Bend, O God! Thy listening ear,
Hear me, O my Father! hear.

Thou, who didst never turn away
   From an humble suppliant's plea,
Wilt Thou Teach me how to pray,
   When I lift my voice to Thee?
Blessed Saviour! good and mild,
Listen to a feeble child.

Saturday.

AVE mercy upon me, O God! according to Thy loving kindness. According unto the multitude of Thy tender mercies blot out my transgressions.

Wash me thoroughly from mine iniquity, and cleanse me from my sin.

For I acknowledge my transgressions : and my sin is ever before me.

Hide Thy face from my sins and blot out all mine iniquities.

Create in me a clean heart, O God! and renew a right spirit within me.—Psalm. li. 1, 2, 3, 9, 10.

Morning Prayer.

DEAR Father in Heaven! hear me this morning while I again offer Thee daily prayer and praise. How

kind and gracious Thou art, to continue
my life and give me so many blessings.
Lord, make me to know that I do not deserve
any good thing of Thee, but Thou dost
give me all out of Thy great love to me.
Give me an humble, thankful love to Thee
for Thy goodness. I cannot repay Thee
for it. Do not let me think I can. I am
only a wicked little child, and Thou art
the great and holy God. I am not good
and cannot do any good, unless Thou help
me. I ask Thee to-day for Thy help. May
Thy grace make me strong to do right and
leave wrong. Let, I pray Thee, a sense of
Thy greatness and holiness fill me with
that fear of Thee which is the beginning
of wisdom. And may Thy great love win
me to love Thee with all my heart. Hear
me also while I ask for Thy blessing on
all my friends and all for whom Thou
wouldst have me pray. For Jesus' sake I
ask it all. Amen.

Evening Prayer.

ANOTHER week has gone, O God! and kept safe from harm by Thy love, I come to seek Thy forgiveness for all the sins of the past, and Thy blessing on the day that is to come. Prepare me for Thy holy day. I thank Thee for all the happy play days of this week. Help me now to put away play till after to-morrow, and be ready for a different kind of happiness. Make the Sabbath a pleasure to me, a happy, happy day. I have great need to ask to be forgiven for all my wickedness. There is no need that I should tell Thee how I have offended Thee. Forgive each sin and take it away from me, I beg of Thee, and make me a true child of Thine. Hear me when I ask Thee again and again for Thy favor. Do not be angry that I come so often, saying every day I have sinned, but save me from sin and from my own wicked heart. Bless

me to-night as Thou seest I need. I give
myself into Thy care. Now I lay me down
to sleep, I pray the Lord my soul to keep.
If I should die before I wake, I pray the
Lord my soul to take. And this I ask for
Jesus' sake. Amen.

Hymn.

LORD, teach a little child to pray,
   And, oh, accept my prayer !
  Thou hearest all the words I say,
   For Thou art everywhere.

Teach me to do whate'er is right,
   And when I sin, forgive,
And make it still my chief delight
   To love Thee while I live.

Whatever trouble I am in
   To Thee for help I'll call ;
But keep me, more than all, from sin,
   For that 's the worst of all.

Third Sunday.

OW upon the first day of the week, very early in the morning, they came unto the sepulchre, bringing the spices which they had prepared, and certain others with them.

And they found the stone rolled away from the sepulchre. And they entered in, and found not the body of the Lord Jesus.

And it came to pass, as they were much perplexed thereabout, behold, two men stood by them in shining garments.

And as they were afraid, and bowed down their faces to the earth, they said unto them, Why seek ye the living among the dead?

He is not here, but is risen.—LUKE xxiv. 1–6.

Morning Prayer.

I THANK Thee, O Lord! that Thou hast spared me to see yet another of Thy holy days. Let Thy blessing rest upon me through all its hours, teaching me to keep it holy, and making it a very happy day to me. Thou dost not give me these Sabbath-days, that I should find them long and tiresome, but that they may be the best and happiest days of my life; days in which I may learn lessons of heavenly love and wisdom. Go with me to-day if I go with Thy people to worship in Thy house. Keep me sober and quiet although I am very happy. Help me to know and understand the message Thou wilt send me to-day. Make me thoughtful and attentive when I read or study the Bible, Thy holy Word, and whether in church, at Sabbath-school, or at home, do Thou be with me and bless me. Bless all for whom I should pray. Bless the whole world and make known Thy love and truth to all who do not serve and love Thee, in Christian lands and in heathen lands, and may sinners this day begin to live in Thy fear. For Thine is the kingdom, the power, and the glory for ever and ever. Amen.

Evening Prayer.

ORD! I come before Thee now seeking for an evening blessing. Thou hast been very kind and loving to me, in granting me another of Thy holy days. Teach me to know aright the worth of these Sabbaths. I pray Thee that this one, which is now closing, may not have been given to me in vain, but that its holy influences may go with me all through this week. May I not forget the lessons of this day when I close my eyes in sleep to-night, but may I keep them in my mind, to act upon every day in the week. Forgive my sins this day, my carelessness and thoughtlessness about keeping it holy to

Thee.   Give me true sorrow and repentance for my wrong doing.   Help me, O God! that I may not say I am sorry, and want Thy pardon while I am thinking other thoughts in my heart.   Bless to-night all those whom I love, and all for whom I should pray.   Do for them more and better than I can ask or think.   May they all be Thy loved and loving children, and live to Thy glory, and Thy great name shall shall have all the praise for ever.   Amen.

Hymn.

OW sweet is the Sabbath to me,
    The day when the Saviour arose;
        'Tis heaven His beauties to see,
And in His soft arms to repose.

This day He invites me to come,
    How kindly He bids me draw near;
He offers me heaven for home,
    And wipes off the penitent tear.

He offers to pardon my sin,
    And keep me from every snare,
To sprinkle and cleanse me within,
    And show me His tenderest care.

Monday.

I F ye love me, keep my commandments :
He that hath my commandments, and
keepeth them, he it is that loveth me :
and he that loveth me, shall be loved of my Father, and I will love him, and will manifest myself to him.

If a man love me he will keep my words : and
my Father will love him, and we will come unto
him, and make our abode with Him.

If ye keep my commandments ye shall abide in
my love.—JOHN xiv. 15, 21, 23 ; xv. 10.

Morning Prayer.

O GOD! my Father in Heaven, Thou
hast kindly spared me to begin another week ; hear me now while I
seek for Thy blessing to go with me through
all its hours. Help me to resolve that with
Thy help I will spend it in Thy fear. I

know that even a little child can live to Thy glory. In Thy holy Word Thou hast said that even such every-day things as eating and drinking, may be done as unto Thee. Teach me, then, to do my little duties and lessons as for Thee. And not only about work and lessons may I seek to serve Thee, but in playtime and with my playmates may I carry about thoughts of Thee. Make me cheerful, obedient and faithful at my tasks. Make me kind, unselfish, gentle and loving in my plays. Show me what to do for Thee. Show me if I can make another happy. Show me how I can be useful and helpful, and give me a willing heart and willing hands to do good for Jesus' sake. Keep me from sin this day. Give me Thy grace to keep me humble, Thy strength to keep me right, Thy love to keep me loving, and I will praise Thee, the only living and true God, now and for ever. Amen.

Evening Prayer.

EFORE I lie down to sleep, O Lord! I come to ask Thy pardon and blessing. I have need every day to ask to be forgiven, for when I do my best I am full of sin, in Thy holy sight, for Thou art so pure and holy that Thou dost hate all sin. Yet hating sin, Thou dost love sinners, and dost bid them come to Thee for pardon and grace, promising to give a new heart to such as ask Thee. Help me to ask Thee aright. For Jesus' sake forgive my sins and make me to hate all that displeases Thee. Bless me to-night with Thy loving care. In the darkness be Thou near me. If it please Thee keep me safe till morning. Then as the only return I can make to Thee for Thy love, help me to give Thee my heart and serve Thee every day. I pray Thee for the same blessings of love and pardon for all whom I

love, and all for whom I should pray.
Teach the whole world to know and love
Jesus Christ, and to serve and praise the
one holy and true God, Father, Son, and
Holy Spirit for ever.   Amen.

Hymn.

ONE there is above all others
    Well deserves the name of Friend;
  His is love beyond a brother's,
Costly, free, and knows no end.

Which of all our friends to save us
    Could or would have shed His blood?
But the Saviour died to have us
    Reconciled in Him to God.

Oh, for grace our hearts to soften,
    Teach us, Lord! at length to love.
We, alas! forget too often
    What a Friend we have above.

Tuesday.

EVERY good gift and every perfect gift is from above, and cometh down from the Father of lights, with whom is no variableness, neither shadow of turning.—JAMES i. 17.

He that spared not His own Son, but delivered Him up for us all, how shall He not with Him also freely give us all things.—ROM. viii. 32.

The young lions do lack, and suffer hunger; but they that seek the Lord shall not want any good thing.—PSALM xxxiv. 10.

Morning Prayer.

I WOULD offer Thee praise and thanksgiving again, O Lord! for all Thy tender mercies toward me. I thank Thee this morning for my home and friends, for the quiet rest of the past night, for food, and clothes, and bed, for life, health and safety. What shall I return unto Thee, O God! for Thy goodness? All that I have Thou hast given me, and the only thing I can give Thee is myself. Take me, dear Jesus! as Thine own. Make me pure and holy that Thou mayest love me. Teach me, O God! my need of Thee and Thy help. When I take the greatest care, I cannot of myself avoid all wrong doing; and when I keep the closest watch, I easily fall into temptation and sin. Do Thou, then, be pleased to undertake for me. Guide me and strengthen me in right ways. Keep me back from sin. Fill my heart with pure and holy desires. Wash me in the blood of Jesus. Bless all my friends, each one as Thou seest the need. Make us all Thy children. Guide us to Thy glory, and save us at last for Jesus' sake. Amen.

Evening Prayer.

DEAR Jesus! wilt Thou not come near to a little child, who now tries to come near to Thee to beg for Thy love, care and forgiveness? O Lord! I am only a little helpless child, but Thou lovest even such as I, and died to save us. Save me, I pray Thee, from sin and its punishment. Take away the love of sinning from my heart. Give me a new heart that shall love and serve Thee. Forgive me all the wrong I have done this day. Remember it not against me, but wash me in Thy blood which cleanseth from all sin. Watch over and care for me through the dark night. If it please Thee send quiet sleep to rest me; and wake me in the morning in health and happiness. Wilt Thou, with me, love and bless all whom I love. Make them all Thy friends. Take care of them through all their lives here in this world, and bring us all together to praise Thee in heaven. I ask it for Jesus' sake. Amen.

Hymn.

SAVIOUR! I am very weak,
   Wilt Thou hear me when I speak?
   May I come and tell Thee all,
Though I am so young and small?

And wilt Thou take my sinful heart
And make it pure in every part?
Help me to grow a loving child,
Like Thee, obedient, meek and mild?

Dear Saviour! be my constant guide,
Nor let me wander from Thy side:
Oh, fit me for Thy home on high,
And take me to Thee when I die!

𝔚ednesday.

SURELY He hath borne our griefs, and carried our sorrows : yet we did esteem Him stricken, smitten of God, and afflicted.

But He was wounded for our transgressions, He was bruised for our iniquities; the chastisement of our peace was upon Him; and with His stripes we are healed.

All we like sheep have gone astray; we have turned every one to his own way; and the Lord hath laid on Him the iniquity of us all.—ISAIAH liii. 4–6.

Morning Prayer.

ALMIGHTY God! who though so great and wise dost take care of all Thy creatures, accept, I pray Thee, the worship of a little child, who has received so many blessings from Thy hand.

When I think of Thy power and holiness, I am afraid to appear before Thee, and it is only because Thou art so full of love, that I dare pray unto Thee. Send down Thy Spirit into my heart to give me that holy fear of Thee that I ought to have, and the love and trust Thou dost deserve. Be with me this day to bless me and keep me in right ways. Supply all my wants as Thou seest best for me. Keep me from harm and sickness; feed and clothe me, and spare me home and friends. Above all, O God! take care of my soul, make it pure and holy, washed white in Jesus' blood; thinking holy, loving thoughts, leading me to obedient, kind and gentle ways. Make me more thoughtful to-day for the happiness and comfort of those around me, than careful to please myself. May I remember to try to please Thee. Hear my prayer for myself, for my dear friends and playmates, and for all for whom Thou wouldst have me pray, and I will give Thee praise and glory for ever. Amen.

Evening Prayer.

O THOU loving Jesus! who didst bless the little ones when Thou wast on the earth, send, I pray, a blessing from above to rest on me to-night. Thou who didst call Thyself the good Shepherd, take me as one of Thy lambs. Keep me in Thy fold and near Thy side. Teach me to know and love Thy voice, and to follow after Thee. Do not be angry with me when I sin and turn away from Thee, but, dear Saviour! call me back to Thee and forgive my sins. Wash me white in Thy blood. Take away the love of sin and sinning from my heart, and give me a new heart that shall love Thee and hate wickedness. Watch over me and all I love this night. Keep us all in peace and safety. Love us, forgive us, and accept us for Thine own name's sake. Amen.

Hymn.

AND is it true what I am told,
   That there are lambs within the fold
     Of God's eternal Son ?
That Jesus Christ with tender care,
Will in His arms most gently bear
   The helpless little one ?

Oh, yes ! I've heard my mother say,
He never sent a child away
   That scarce could walk or run ;
For when the parent love besought
That He would bless the child she brought,
   He blessed the little one.

And I, a little straying lamb,
May come to Jesus as I am,
   Though goodness I have none ;
May now be folded to His breast,
As birds within the parent nest,
   And be His little one.

Thursday.

T HOU, God! seest me.—GEN. xvi. 13.

The eyes of the Lord are in every place, beholding the evil and the good. —PROV. xv. 3.

Am I a God at hand, saith the Lord, and not a God afar off?

Can any hide himself in secret places that I shall not see him? saith the Lord. Do not I fill heaven and earth? saith the Lord.—JER. xxiii. 23, 24.

Morning Prayer.

G REAT and holy Lord God! who hast made all things, and without whom was not anything made that was made, teach me Thy greatness and holiness as well as Thy love and goodness, as I come before Thee now to pray for Thy daily blessing. And may I know and feel this not only now, but all the day long. Make me glad to know that wherever I go Thou goest; That Thou seest all I do, and knowest all I say or think. Send Thy Holy Spirit, I pray Thee, to stay in my heart; to make me pure and well-pleasing in Thy sight. Guard me from danger and keep me from sin this day. Make me gentle and kind in my plays; faithful and obedient at my work and lessons. Take away all evil passions from my heart, and keep my lips that they may speak no wrong or unkind words. Wash my soul in the blood of Jesus, clothe me with His righteousness, and fit me for His service for Jesus' sake. Amen.

Evening Prayer.

O LORD! fill my heart with thankfulness, I pray Thee, for all the blessings I receive. All I have comes from Thee. Thou only dost keep me in life, health and safety. If Thou shouldst forget me for one minute I should die, for I cannot keep my own life, or supply my own needs. Teach me this more perfectly, Heavenly Father! that so I may be humble as well as grateful for Thy care over me. Teach me my own sinfulness, helplessness and danger, and make me to know and understand Thy willingness and power to save me from sin and death. Give me grace to receive, love and obey the Saviour Thou hast sent to save sinners. Forgive my many sins, and make sin hateful to me. Bless, I pray Thee, all whom I love, and all for whom I should pray. Do for each one just what Thou knowest best and needful. Make us all Thy friends, and for Thine own name's sake, save us with Thee in heaven, and the praise and glory shall be Thine for ever. Amen.

6

Hymn.

LORD, look upon a little child,
  By nature sinful, rude and wild;
  Oh, let Thy grace descend on me,
And make me all I ought to be:

Make me Thy child—a child of God,
Washed in the Saviour's precious blood;
And my whole heart from sin set free,
A little vessel full of Thee.

Dear Saviour! take me to Thy breast,
And bless me that I may be blest;
Both when I wake and when I sleep,
Thy little lamb in safety keep.

Friday.

STAND therefore, having your loins girt about with truth, and having on the breast-plate of righteousness ;

And your feet shod with the preparation of the Gospel of peace ;

Above all, taking the shield of faith, wherewith ye shall be able to quench all the fiery darts of the wicked.

And take the helmet of salvation, and the sword of the Spirit, which is the Word of God :

Praying always with all prayer and supplication in the Spirit.—EPH. vi. 14–18.

Morning Prayer.

HEAVENLY Father ! again I come to Thee to offer my daily prayer, and ask for Thy blessing upon me and all whom I love. Teach me how to pray and what to pray for. Put right desires into my mind, and right feelings into my heart. Make me one of Thine own little ones. Create in me a clean heart, and make me to grow every day more and more like Jesus, who served Thee perfectly when He was a little child upon earth. And while I ask Thee to do this for me, help me to remember that I have something to do myself. Keep me ever watchful against evil, and careful to do right. Let Thy blessing rest upon me to-day wherever I am and whatever doing. Feed me, clothe me, and give me comfort and happiness, if it please Thee. Give me a thankful heart for all Thy blessings. Lead me and take care of me this day and every day, and fit me for Thy home, when my life shall end. For Jesus' sake I ask it. Amen.

Evening Prayer.

T is of Thy mercy, O Lord! that I am spared through the dangers, seen and unseen, of another day. How great is Thy loving kindness toward me. How constant is Thy watchful care! Thy hand has been about me for good all my life long. Surely goodness and mercy from the Lord follow me in all my ways. What return ought I to make Thee for these favors, but what a return *do* I make Thee. I would humbly confess my sins before Thee this night. I do many things I ought not to do, and leave undone much that I ought to do. Sin is in all my thoughts, words and deeds. I am full of unholiness. Merciful Saviour! pity me in my unrighteousness, and clothe me with Thy righteousness. Thou who wast made sin for sinners, and died that they might be forgiven and live, I come to Thee to be made pure and holy, to be loved and forgiven. Send me not away, but receive and bless me for Thine own name's sake. Amen.

Hymn.

I KNOW 't is Jesus loves my soul,
And makes the wounded spirit whole;
  My nature is by sin defiled,
Yet Jesus loves a little child.

How kind is Jesus, oh, how good!
'T was for my soul He shed His blood;
For children's sake He was reviled,
For Jesus loves a little child.

When I offend by thought or tongue,
Omit the right, or do the wrong,
If I repent He 's reconciled,
For Jesus loves a little child.

To me may Jesus now impart,
Although so young, a gracious heart;
Alas! I 'm oft by sin defiled,
Yet Jesus loves a little child.

Saturday.

GAIN I say unto you, that if two of you shall agree on earth, as touching anything that they shall ask, it shall be done for them of my Father which is in heaven.—MATT. xviii. 19.

And I say unto you, Ask, and it shall be given you; seek, and ye shall find; knock, and it shall be opened unto you.

For every one that asketh, receiveth; and he that seeketh, findeth; and to him that knocketh, it shall be opened.—LUKE xi. 9, 10.

And this is the confidence that we have in Him, that if we ask anything according to His will, He heareth us.—1 JOHN v. 14.

Morning Prayer.

HEAVENLY Father! make my mind solemn and my heart sincere, while I come to offer Thee my daily worship. Put right desires into my heart and right words upon my lips, that my worship may please Thee and bring down Thy blessing. I thank Thee for the mercies of the past night. For a dear home and friends, for quiet rest and sleep. I ask Thee to help me to serve Thee while I am awake, to keep Thy fear and love in my heart. My Father! wilt Thou not be the guide of my youth? Fill my heart with Thy love. Make me strong to choose the right when tempted. Keep me from evil. Wash me in that blood which cleanseth from all sin. Bless me with such mercies as Thou art willing I should have, and make me thankful for all Thou givest me. Bless all my dear friends and keep them in peace and safety. Bless the whole world. May Thy kingdom come, and Thy will be done, for Thine is the kingdom, the power and the glory, for ever. Amen.

Evening Prayer.

EAR Jesus! tender Saviour! I come to Thee to-night a little tired, sleepy child, waiting only for Thy blessing before I go to sleep. Thy care has been around me all day. Safe in Thy keeping I have gone about in the midst of dangers, seen and unseen, and now I am alive, unhurt, with many blessings, because Thou hast not once forgotten me. Forgive me that I have forgotten Thee. Cleanse me from all my sins. Take away their guilt; make me to hate them, and love holiness. I give myself to Thee to-night. Keep me still under Thy loving care. If it please Thee give me sweet rest and sleep, and wake me in the morning a happy child. Make me very thankful for all Thy love to me. Teach me to love Thee best of all, and to live to Thy glory. Sleeping or waking, living or dying, make me all Thine, and all my friends Thine too, for Thine is the kingdom, the power and the glory, for ever and ever. Amen.

Hymn.

JESUS, tender Saviour!
  Hast Thou died for me?
Make me very thankful
In my heart to Thee.
  When the sad, sad story
Of Thy grief I read,
  Make me very sorry
For my sins indeed.

Now I know Thou lovest
  And dost plead for me;
Make me very thankful
  In my prayer to Thee.
Soon I hope in glory
  At Thy side to stand;
Make me meet to see Thee
  In that happy land.

Fourth Sunday.

IF thou turn away thy foot from the Sabbath, from doing thy pleasure on my holy day; and call the Sabbath a delight, the holy of the Lord, honorable; and shalt honor Him, not doing thine own ways, nor finding thine own pleasure, nor speaking thine own words:

Then shalt thou delight thyself in the Lord; and I will cause thee to ride upon the high places of the earth, and feed thee with the heritage of Jacob thy father, for the mouth of the Lord hath spoken it.—Is. lviii. 13, 14.

Morning Prayer.

I BLESS Thee, O God! for the light of another holy Sabbath. This is Thy day, help me to keep it in Thy fear. I would begin the day by lifting up my voice in praise to Thee for all Thy goodness and love. Especially do I praise

Thee to-day for Thy holy Word. That Thou hast made it so plain and free. That it not only makes known Thy law and Thy holiness, but tells of Thy love and salvation. I thank Thee, O my Heavenly Father! that there are words and messages in it for little children. Help me to-day to open my heart to these words of Thine; to keep and practise them in my life, and to believe them with all my heart. Be very near to-day to all Thy people. Send Thy Holy Spirit to be in all Thy churches, and to show Thy love to sinners that they may turn from their evil ways. May the love of Jesus Christ be spread through all the earth, and the time soon come when all shall know, and love, and serve the only true God. Amen.

Evening Prayer.

BOW down Thine ear, O God! and hear my evening prayer. Thou art the only wise and true God, yet though Thou art high and lifted up above all beings, Thou dost delight in the praise and worship even of little children. Help me to worship Thee in spirit and in truth. I thank Thee to-night for the blessings and privileges of another Sunday. I have not been as careful as I ought to keep it holy unto Thee, yet grant, I beseech of Thee, that some good may remain with me from its holy hours and services. May I be a better and happier child all through the week that is to come, for having had this quiet, holy day. Forgive all my sins, whether of thought, word or deed. Have mercy upon me, O God! according to Thy loving kindness. Wash me from my sins. Cover my wickedness with the robe of Christ's righteousness. Make me to hate evil and to strive after good. Thus may I love and serve Thee while I live, and glorify and enjoy Thee for ever. In the name and for the sake of the dear Lord Jesus. I ask it. Amen.

Hymn.

WELCOME, welcome, day of rest,
    To the world in kindness given,
    Welcome to this humble breast,
As the beaming light from heaven.

Day of tidings from the skies,
    Day of solemn praise and prayer,
Day to make the simple wise,
    Oh, how great Thy blessings are !

Welcome, welcome, day of rest,
    With Thy influence all divine ;
May Thy hallowed hours be blest
    To this feeble heart of mine.

Monday.

I AM the good shepherd : the good shepherd giveth His life for the sheep.

I am the good shepherd, and know my sheep, and am known of mine. JOHN X. 11, 14.

He shall feed His flock like a shepherd : He shall gather the lambs with His arm, and carry them in His bosom, and shall gently lead those that are with young.—Is. xl. 11.

Morning Prayer.

LET Thy blessing rest upon me, Heavenly Father ! as I lift up my voice in prayer to Thee. Teach me to pray with my heart as well as with my voice. I come to ask Thee to watch over and care for me this day, as Thou hast in days gone by. I do not mean only that Thou wilt keep me alive, in health and safety, but that Thou wilt keep my heart; that Thou wilt lead me into right ways and save me from sin. Give me grace to be obedient, faithful, true, gentle and loving. Help me to perform all duties and tasks cheerfully, promptly and well. Make me kind and unselfish in my plays. Help me to give up my own wishes and pleasures, if by so doing I can make another happy. Give me Thy grace in my heart, that I may do these things not to be seen and praised of men, but because they are well-pleasing in Thy sight. Forgive all my sins; wash away all their stains. Love me, bless me, and save me at last in Thy kingdom for the dear Saviour's sake. Amen.

Evening Prayer.

THE day is past and gone, and the still, dark night is coming. Thou hast cared for me all day, Heavenly Father! do Thou still keep a loving watch over me. Keep me safe this night;

safe from sickness, danger and death. Trusting in Thy love, resting in Thy power, may I sleep a quiet, refreshing sleep. Wake me in the morning, if it seem good to Thee, in health and happiness. But not only for Thy watchful care would I pray to Thee, O God! but that Thou wouldst pardon my many sins. I beg Thee, for Thy dear Son's sake, not to remember my sin against me; not to keep Thine anger against me, but to be at peace with me, because Jesus died for sinners such as I am. I commend to Thee for Thy blessing all for whom I should pray, everywhere, for Thou art a great God, and in every place. Grant Thy favor to all whom I love. Bless the whole world. Fill it with holiness and love. Make it Thine own kingdom, and to the Father, Son and Holy Spirit, shall be all praise for ever. Amen.

7

Hymn.

I AM Jesus' little lamb,
Therefore glad and gay I am;
Jesus loves me, Jesus knows me,
All that 's good and fair He shows me,
Tends me every day the same,
Even calls me by my name.

Should not I be glad and gay,
In this blessed fold all day ?
By this Holy Shepherd tended,
Whose kind arms, when life is ended,
Bear me to the world of light ?
Yes ! oh, yes, my lot is bright !

Tuesday.

THOU shalt love the Lord thy God with all thy heart, and with all thy soul, and with all thy mind.

This is the first and great commandment.

And the second is like unto it. Thou shalt love thy neighbor as thyself.

On these two commandments hang all the law and the prophets.—MATT. xxii. 37–40.

Morning Prayer.

O LORD! now when I come to say my daily prayer to Thee, help me to remember, Thou, God! seest me, Thou dost not only hear the words I speak, but dost know whether I mean them in my heart. Teach me how to pray and what to pray for. Send, I pray Thee, Thy Holy Spirit into my heart, so to fill it with right and holy feelings that there shall be no room for wickedness. Guide me to-day in Thy fear. Make me a good child; faithful, obedient and truthful. Make me to be attentive to my lessons. While from my parents and teachers I am learning daily lessons, do Thou teach me the beginning of wisdom, which is Thy fear. While I fear Thee, teach me, too, to love Thee for Thy great love with which Thou hast loved me. Lead me not into temptation, but deliver me from evil. Forgive all my sins for Jesus' sake. Love and bless all for whom I should pray. Take me and mine into Thy holy keeping. Make us all Thy friends, and so loving and serving Thee, may we live to Thy praise and enjoy Thee for ever. Amen.

Evening Prayer.

OUR Father who art in heaven, Thou hast kept me in safety through another day, and now at its close, I come seeking Thy forgiveness for my wicked ways, and praying Thee to continue Thy loving care over me. O Lord! I have forgotten Thee, but Thou hast not forgotten me. I have done wrong in many different ways, and have not taken care to serve Thee in all my deeds. For Jesus' sake I beg Thee to forgive these my sins, and not only forgive them, but help me to watch against them, and to put them away from me. I am very poor and weak. I cannot make myself any better. Do Thou be strong for me, and make me holy and pure. Show me myself, but oh, show me Thyself too, and teach me to love Thee, because Thou didst first love me. Bless to-night all for whom I should pray. Do good unto all my friends, and bless them with Thy love. Now I lay me down to sleep, I pray the Lord my soul to keep. If I should die before I wake, I pray the Lord my soul to take. And this I ask for Jesus' sake. Amen.

Hymn.

OUR Father in heaven,
  We hallow Thy name!
May Thy kingdom holy
On earth be the same!
Oh, give to us daily
  Our portion of bread,
It is from Thy bounty
  That all must be fed.

Forgive our transgressions,
  And teach us to know
That humble compassion
  That pardons each foe;
Keep us from temptation,
  From weakness and sin,
And Thine be the glory
  Forever.   Amen.

Wednesday.

OME now, and let us reason together, saith the Lord : though your sins be as scarlet, they shall be as white as snow ; though they be red like crimson, they shall be as wool.—Is. i. 18.

Ho, every one that thirsteth, come ye to the waters ; and he that hath no money, come ye, buy, and eat ; yea, come, buy wine and milk without money and without price.—Is. lv. 1.

And the Spirit and the bride say, Come. And let him that heareth say, Come. And let him that is athirst come. And whosoever will, let him take the water of life freely.—Rev. xxii. 17.

Morning Prayer.

ET again have I to thank Thee, Father in heaven, for a new day. I come to ask Thee to go with me through its hours, that I may spend them

in Thy fear.   O Lord! I am only a little
child, but I am not too young to love Thee
and live to Thy glory.   I am very weak,
but Thou art very strong.   Help me, I
pray Thee, whenever I need help.   I am
full of sin, Thou didst never sin, but dost
hate it, yet Thou didst give Thy dear Son
to die to save sinners.   I am a sinner, wash
me clean in Christ's blood.   Teach me to
hate every evil way.   Save me from sin
and its punishment.   Make me a good
child to-day, truthful, obedient, faithful,
kind.   Show me what to do for Jesus.
Let me never be ashamed to be known as
a lamb of His fold, but be ever careful to
please Him in all my ways, and anxious to
help others to serve Him too.   Put right
desires into my heart and lead me in Thy
paths.   Hear my prayer and answer it for
Christ's sake.   Amen.

Evening Prayer.

COME down into my heart, Thou gentle Spirit of God, and take away all naughty passions and sinful thoughts before I go to rest for another night. Let me be afraid to go to sleep with anger or disobedience in my heart. Thou art all love, and meekness, and holiness, come and dwell in me that I may be like Thee. Teach me the holy lessons I need to learn. Be very patient with me if I am dull or careless about learning them, and give me Thy grace to make me wise unto salvation. I ask Thee to-night, O God! for a loving, unselfish heart, a heart that shall love Thee more and better than all the world beside, and ready to love all who need my love. Not only those who love me and make it easy for me to love them, but all others. Dear Jesus! Thou dost know how hard it is to love and pray for unkind and selfish people, help

me to do just as Thou wouldst have me
when I meet with those who seem so to
me. As I ask Thee to forgive me, so may
I be willing to forgive all who offend me.
Bless, love, keep and save me, for Thy
name's sake. Amen.

Hymn.

I WANT to be like Jesus,
 So lowly and so meek ;
For no one marked an angry word
 That ever heard Him speak.

I want to be like Jesus,
 So frequently in prayer ;
Alone upon the mountain top
 He met His Father there.

I want to be like Jesus,
 Engaged in doing good,
So that of me it may be said,
 " She hath done what she could."

Alas ! I'm not like Jesus,
 As any one may see ;
O gentle Saviour ! send Thy grace,
 And make me like to Thee.

Thursday.

B E sober, be vigilant; because your adversary, the devil, as a roaring lion, walketh about, seeking whom he may devour.

Whom resist steadfast in the faith.—1 Peter v. 8, 9.

Resist the devil and he will flee from you.—James iv. 7.

There hath no temptation taken you but such as is common to man: but God is faithful, who will not suffer you to be tempted above that ye are able; but will with the temptation also make a way to escape, that ye may be able to bear it. —1 Cor. x. 13.

Morning Prayer.

T HY goodness and mercy, Heavenly Father! follow me every day of my life. I lie down and sleep, and in the dark, while I am helpless and know nothing of danger, Thou dost keep me safely in Thy care. I wake to find the same blessings Thou hast given me all my life, yet new, and waiting for me; life, health, food, clothing, home, friends. Every good thing I have comes from Thee. I cannot count Thy gifts to me. Why art Thou so merciful and good? Not because I deserve it, for, O Lord! I am a sinner in Thy sight, and Thou canst not bear sin. Not because I can merit it, for when I do my best I cannot keep all Thy law. It is not for anything in myself that Thou dost give me so many mercies, but because Thou art love, because Jesus died for sinners. Loving God! give me yet more, I pray Thee, even a thankful heart, a new heart, and for Thy dear Son's sake, forgiveness of sin. Guide me, O Lord! in wisdom's ways, and at last bring me to Thy heavenly home for Jesus' sake. Amen.

Evening Prayer.

BEFORE I sleep, I would ask again, dear Jesus! that Thy love may follow me yet as it has through all my life. I come to give myself into Thy care for another night. In the darkness be Thou near me; when I sleep, do Thou please to watch over me. Refresh me with peaceful sleep, and wake me in the morning in health and happiness, if it be Thy will. But this is not the only blessing I would ask of Thee, Thou loving Saviour! who didst die to save sinners. Every day I have need to ask Thee to forgive my sins. Lord! art Thou tired of this my daily prayer? Art Thou angry that I sin so often? I know Thou art grieved at every wicked way, but I do pray Thee yet again to forgive and love me. Make me to see sin as Thou seest it. Teach me Thy love to me, then shall I love Thee and hate sin. Help me to ask this with my whole heart. Bless and keep all my dear friends. I ask all in Jesus' name and for His sake only. Amen.

Hymn.

JESUS ! to Thy dear arms I flee,
I have no other help but Thee ;
For Thou dost suffer me to come,
Oh, take a little wanderer home !

Jesus, I cannot see Thee here,
Yet still I know Thou 'rt very near ;
Oh, say my sins are all forgiven,
And I shall dwell with Thee in heaven !

And now, dear Jesus ! I am Thine,
Oh, be Thou ever, ever mine !
And let me never, never roam,
From Thee, the little wanderer's home.

Friday.

THIS is a faithful saying, and worthy of all acceptation, that Christ Jesus came into the world to save sinners.—1 TIM. i. 15.

Who His own self bare our sins in His own body on the tree, that we, being dead to sins, should live unto righteousness.—1 PET. ii. 24.

For the Son of man is come to seek and to save that which was lost.—LUKE xix. 10.

Neither is there salvation in any other: for there is none other name under heaven given among men, whereby we must be saved.—ACTS iv. 12.

Morning Prayer.

COME near to me, Thou blessed Saviour! while I try to worship Thee. Fill my heart with praise and thanks to Thee for the blessings of this day. O Lord! Thou dost fill my life with good things. I cannot count all Thy mercies toward me, a weak, helpless, sinful child. I would lift up my voice and heart in praise to Thee for Thy goodness. Grant, I pray Thee, while Thou art giving me all these blessings, that greatest blessing, pardon for my sins, with Thy love and peace in my heart. Dear Jesus! I am sinning against Thee every day and many times a day. Every day I have as much need as ever before to seek Thy forgiveness. Even when I want to do good, I do much wrong. I have no strength to get the better of all the evil passions in my heart. What can I do but come to Thee and beg Thee to forgive my sins, and to fight with me against them. Give me a new heart, I beg of Thee, and help me to seek after holiness. Take me into Thy fold. Accept of me, and save me for Thy great love's sake. Amen.

Evening Prayer.

NOTHER day is gone, and what do I wait for now, O Lord! but Thy blessing. Thou hast kindly kept me in safety thus far, and I ask Thee to continue Thy care and watch over me while I sleep. I cannot take care of myself, but Thou dost never sleep. The darkness is the same as the light to Thee. To Thy care I commit myself. What time I am afraid I will trust in Thee, for Thou only makest me to dwell in safety. And while Thou art caring for my body, care too for my soul. I give it to Thee to keep. Make it pure and holy that Thou mayest love me. Forgive, I pray Thee, for Thy dear Son's sake, all my sins. Take away from me the love of sinning, and give me love to Thee. I pray to Thee for all my friends, my parents, brothers, sisters and playmates, and for the world. Love them

all, and bless each one, as Thou seest the
need to be.　Save us all to praise Thee for
ever.　Amen.

Hymn.

JUST as I am—without one plea,
But that Thy blood was shed for me,
And that Thou bid'st me come to Thee,
O Lamb of God! I come.

Just as I am—and waiting not
To rid my soul of one dark blot,
To Thee whose blood can cleanse each spot,
O Lamb of God! I come.

Just as I am—Thou wilt receive;
Wilt welcome, pardon, cleanse, relieve;
Because Thy promise I believe,
O Lamb of God! I come.

Saturday.

COME unto me, all ye that labor and are heavy laden, and I will give you rest.

Take my yoke upon you, and learn of me: for I am meek and lowly in heart; and ye shall find rest unto your souls.

For my yoke is easy, and my burden is light. MATT. xi. 28–30.

And him that cometh to me, I will in no wise cast out.—JOHN vi. 37.

Morning Prayer.

HEAVENLY Father! listen while I cry unto Thee. Teach me how to pray and what to pray for. I offer Thee praise and thanksgiving for all Thy goodness to me, a sinful child. I thank Thee for Thy countless blessings given me so freely every day. I praise Thee for Thy wonderful love in giving Thine only Son

to die to save sinners. Save me, I pray
Thee, for His sake. My heart is very
wicked and full of sin. I cannot make
it clean or good. I·come to Thee just as
I am. Take me, dear Jesus! and make
me holy. Teach me Thy truth, and lead
me in Thy ways. Make it the great desire
of my heart to please Thee. Keep me in
Thy fear and love. Bless me to-day with
such good as Thou seest best for me, and
make me thankful and contented. For
Jesus' sake hear and answer my prayer.
Amen.

Evening Prayer.

PUT far from me, O God! all noisy
ways and thoughtless feelings, as I
try to worship Thee at the close of
another day. May I not only say my prayers, but may I pray in my heart. May I
stop and think what the words I say mean,
for if I idly and carelessly repeat them, I
am sinning against Thee, and deserving
Thy anger. I come to Thee every day for

Thy blessing, help and forgiveness, for every day I have new need of Thy love and grace. Show me, I pray Thee, how much I need Thee. Show me my own sinful, helpless heart. Create in me a clean heart, O God! and renew a right spirit within me. Wash me clean in the blood of the Lamb, which cleanseth from all sin. Keep me and all I love in Thy kind keeping, this night and all our lives. I ask it all for Jesus' sake. Amen.

Hymn.

OFTEN say my prayers,
 But do I ever pray?
Or do the wishes of my heart,
Suggest the words I say?

'T is useless to implore
 Unless I feel my need—
Unless 't is from a sense of want
 That all my prayers proceed.

Lord, teach me what I want,
 And teach me how to pray:
Nor let me e'er implore Thy grace
 Not feeling what I say.

Occasional Prayers.

For a Sick Child.

KIND and tender Jesus, who didst heal many sick children when Thou wast on earth, listen to my prayer as I cry unto Thee. If it be Thy will, cure me, and take away this pain and suffering. If not, please help me to bear it patiently. Support me with the thought of Thy rich love, and grant me Thy loving favor. Forgive all my sins, and remember them no more against me for ever, for Thy name's sake. Amen.

For a Sick Child.

FATHER in heaven! look down in mercy and love upon a sick child. I am weak, and tired, and suffering; if it please Thee, heal all my sick-

ness, soothe my pains, and give me anew
health and strength. O Thou strong, loving and patient God ! do Thou undertake
for me and grant me the grace I need to
make me patient, humble and obedient
under my pain and restlessness. Forgive
me, love me and help me ; and, oh, cure
my soul of the worse sickness of sin, and
accept of me as Thine for Christ's sake.
Amen.

For a Birthday.

THOU hast added one more year to
my life, O God ! and now I come
before Thee, to offer thanks for the
past, and to seek Thy blessing on the fu-
ture. When I remember the past, how
great has been Thy goodness toward me !
Truly my blessings have been more than
I can count, and Thy loving kindnesses
toward me have been new every day. Fill
my heart with grateful love for these, Thy
mercies, and godly sorrow that I have
made Thee such a return of sin and dis-

obedience. O Thou holy God! for the sake of Thy dear Son forgive all the sin that is in me. Wash me in His blood till I am white and pure in Thy sight, and put on me the robe of His righteousness. In mercy grant me much of Thy grace in my heart to enable me to live more in Thy fear, and to walk in the ways of Thy commandments, in this new year of my life. As I grow older in years, may I grow in heavenly wisdom and in favor with God. Teach me to know the importance of life as a time in which to seek and serve Thee, and to prepare for that eternity which I cannot understand, but in which my soul will live for ever. Continue to me, in Thy rich love, all the good things that have made my life so happy and pleasant. Bless me in all my ways, love me, guide me, keep me, and fit me for Thy service, both here and in heaven. In Jesus' name I ask it. Amen.

For Christmas.

O Thee, O blessed Saviour! do I lift up my praise on this day in which is kept the memory of Thy birth on earth. To Thee do I offer a song of thanks that Thou didst so love men as to become a man, that Thou didst so love little children as to be born a babe. O Thou dear Christ-child! now God and King in heaven, is there not room in Thy loving heart for little ones like me? Thou who wast once a little child, dost Thou not know what little children want? Thou who art almighty wilt Thou not help, love and save weak and tiny children? I know, I am sure that Thou art as loving, kind, helpful, as Thou art great, wise and holy. I come to Thee, then, telling Thee of Thy love, calling Thee the Good Shepherd, ever tender of the lambs, and beg Thee to open my heart to receive Thy love; to make me such a little lamb of Thy flock as Thou shalt love to own and bless; to pardon all my sins for Thy name's sake.

Bless all little ones on this Thy day, and their day. Send love and happiness into all little hearts, and oh, be very pitiful and kind to the poor children who have not many friends and comforts. Send them earthly friends, and make them glad this day in the gift of Thyself as their Friend and Saviour. And to Thy name shall be great praise for ever. Amen.

For New Year.

A NEW year calls for a new offering of praise and prayer to Thee, O God! the giver of every good and blessing. I thank Thee for all Thy loving care and mercy so freely given to me in the year just gone. I thank Thee that life and health, home and friends have been spared to me, that so much of love, peace and comfort has surrounded me. Give me some knowledge of what I owe to Thee for such love and mercy, and make me loving and obedient to Thee in all my ways. Make this new year indeed a happy one to me and my friends. If it please Thee, grant me still the same blessings I have so long enjoyed. More than all, let the sweet influences of Thy Holy Spirit fill my heart with much love to Thy dear Son, and lead me into holy ways. So may I become every day more like a child of God, holy, gentle, kind and true.

Bless all whom I love and all for whom I should pray. Send a happy new year to all sick, sad and suffering ones, and grant that many dear children may count this as the happy year in which they learned to hope in Jesus as their dear Saviour. So prepare us all for a happy new year, that shall never end, in heaven, where we shall give glory, honor and praise to Father, Son, and Holy Ghost for ever. Amen.

www.ingramcontent.com/pod-product-compliance
Lightning Source LLC
Chambersburg PA
CBHW030621270326
41927CB00007B/1270